BROOCHES

20 CREATIVE PROJECTS

CORINNE ALAGILLE

Photographs: Frédéric Lucano
Stylist: Corinne Alagille

INTRODUCTION

Make a huge range of brooches from everyday materials:
a piece of fabric, a few coloured pencils, scrap paper, or
other leftover objects you might find lying around in the
bottom of a drawer. Feel free to experiment with these ideas
as your mood takes you. Conjure up unlikely combinations,
and if you are missing one particular element - a specific
type of fabric, say - try looking around for something that
could replace it (decorative paper, for example). In short,
don't be afraid to bring together different materials,
techniques and motifs, and let your imagination run wild!

CONTENTS

TIPS & TECHNIQUES

You will need to use a variety of techniques to make these brooches, with different levels of difficulty.

Wool for felting

To make your own felt, you need carded wool, which is wool that has not been spun into yarn. It is generally sold in small bundles called batts, in a range of pretty colours. Do not cut pieces of carded wool - instead, pull off a clump that's big enough to make the shape you need.

How to needle-felt

Put the wool on a sheet of foam and start to jab it with a felting needle. The idea is to tangle the fibres by jabbing them, making the wool thicker but also reducing its volume. Jab right down into the foam base, but make sure to move the wool from time to time otherwise it will get caught up in the foam.

Work from the outside inwards until you notice the wool starting to become denser. At this point, squeeze and shape the wool with your hands, then leave it to settle before continuing. Avoid making scooping movements through the wool as they could break the needle: instead, make a clean jab, then withdraw the needle to make another jab close by.

Copying a template onto a support with tracing paper

Trace the motif with a soft pencil, then turn over the drawing and go over the lines on the other side. Place this underside of the original tracing on the support and then go over the drawing one more time. The soft graphite will rub off onto the support, leaving the shape you need.

How to use an image transfer medium such as Transcryl®

Transcryl® is a water-based product that allows you to transfer an image printed on unglazed paper onto another support. Apply several coats of the image transfer medium to your image with a paintbrush, allowing it to dry between each coat. Paint beyond the edges of the motif so that the film acquires an even thickness. Leave to dry for at least 24 hours, then cut out your motif. Put it into warm water and peel the paper off the back of the image, which has now been transferred onto a clear film. The image can now be glued in place on a brooch.

Working with crimp beads

Crimp beads are made of soft metal. They can be fixed to another material, or used to join two different materials together (such as wire on a metal ring).

How to use crimp beads

Thread wire through a crimp bead and then squeeze the latter with pointed pliers. The bead will be squashed and thus stay in place on the wire (or on two wires, if the bead is being used to hold them together).

Using a bone folder

A bone folder or paper creaser is a small but handy tool that helps you to make a sharp crease in paper or cardboard. All you have to do is slide the folder (with the help of a ruler) over your support two or three times, to make a pronounced crease. It is then easy to fold thick paper or cardboard without tearing it. There are two types of fold:

- A valley fold, which is folded inwards.
- A mountain fold, which is folded outwards.

How to crochet a chain

Make a slip knot by winding the yarn round the crochet needle and then bringing it through the loop. To make a chain, pass the yarn up and over the needle and then bring it through the loop. Repeat this process until you obtain the desired number of stitches.

PINWHEEL BROOCH

Level of difficulty
Medium

Time required
45 mins

Technique
Ironing + sewing

Materials
2 pieces of iron-on
  interfacing, each
  15 × 15 cm
Fabric glue
1 piece of geometric print
  fabric, 15 × 15 cm
1 piece of plain green
  satin, 15 × 15 cm
1 green or red sequin
1 brooch clip, 2.5 or 3 cm
  long
Iron
Rotary fabric cutter
Ruler
Pencil
Fine paintbrush
Needle + cotton thread
  to match the fabric

Be bold when combining fabrics: mix plain with prints and try to create interesting colour contrasts.

Instructions

1. Measure a 6 × 6 cm square of iron-on interfacing and then cut it out. Place it on the reverse side of the geometric print fabric and use the iron to bond them together.

2. Mark an 8 × 8 cm square around the iron-on fabric, leaving a border of 2 cm of the print fabric all around the edge. Cut out the square.

3. Cut off the corners of the outer fabric, leaving a 2 mm space before each corner of the interfacing (to prevent the corner from fraying), as shown in diagram **Ⓐ**.

4. Apply fabric glue to all the edges of the square of print fabric and fold them down over the interfacing, as shown in diagram **Ⓑ**. Press firmly.

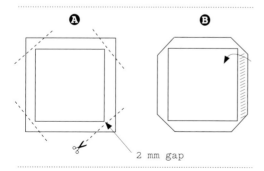

Ⓐ   Ⓑ

2 mm gap

PINWHEEL BROOCH

(continued)

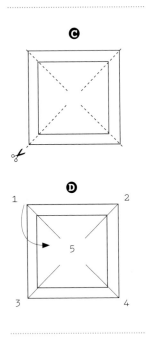

5. Repeat stages 1 to 4, this time beginning with a 5.8 × 5.8 cm square of iron-on interfacing and the plain fabric.

6. Join the two print and plain squares together: apply glue to the back of the plain square and place it in the middle of the square with the geometric design. There should be a 2-mm border around the plain square, allowing the print fabric to show. Press firmly so that the two squares of fabric are well stuck together.

7. Mark the diagonals of this square, then cut along them with a rotary cutter, stopping 1 cm from the centre, as shown in diagram **C**. This will turn each side of the square into a triangular flap.

8. Use the paintbrush to apply a little glue to the edge of the cut sections to stop them from fraying (the glue will turn transparent when it dries). Fold the left-hand corner of each triangular side flap into the centre as shown in diagram **D**: fold 1 onto 5, 2 onto 5, 3 onto 5 and then 4 onto 5.

9. Stitch down all four folded corners into the centre of the square, using the needle and thread.

10. Glue the sequin onto the centre of the pinwheel to hide the stitching, then sew the brooch clip onto the back of the pinwheel.

MOUSTACHE BROOCH

Level of difficulty
Easy

Time required
15 mins

Technique
Sewing + embroidery

Materials
Grey felt
Black wool fabric
Chalk
Sewing scissors
Yellow mercerized cotton
  thread
Embroidery needle
Brooch clip, 4 cm long
Black cotton thread

These witty moustaches look good on anyone.

Instructions

1. Trace the moustache motif from page 68 onto paper and cut it out. Draw round its outline with chalk on both the felt and the black fabric, then cut out both shapes.

2. Thread the needle with yellow thread, then embroider your chosen design from the three illustrated in diagram Ⓐ onto the felt shape.

3. To make the speckled design, pull the needle through from the back of the felt and then push it back through 3 mm away. Repeat this process to create a pattern of tiny stitches going in all directions, as shown in the diagram. For all of the designs, be sure to leave a 5-mm border around the entire edge of the moustache.

4. Cover the back of the felt moustache with the black fabric moustache, then sew them together with the black thread.

5. Sew the brooch clip onto the black fabric backing.

Ⓐ

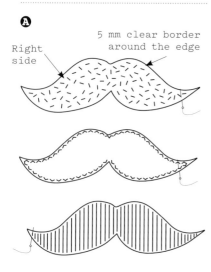

Right side

5 mm clear border around the edge

CLOUD BROOCH

Level of difficulty
Easy

Time required
1 hr + drying time

Technique
Felting

Materials
White carded wool for
  felting
Soap
Scissors
Fine felting needle
Red or pale blue carded
  wool (depending on your
  chosen design)
Red or pale blue thread
  (depending on your
  chosen design)
1 brooch clip, 4 cm long
Sewing needle

This little cloud with its colourful raindrops is guaranteed to liven up any sweater.

Instructions

1. Start by making felt for the cloud: tear off a piece of white carded wool and shape it to form an even mass.

2. Place the wool on a waterproof tray or the edge of a sink, pour a little hot water over it, then rub it with the soap. As the water is pressed out, the wool fibres will tangle together and the wool will shrink and turn into felt. Repeat the process of adding water, rubbing with soap and pressing out the water, until you obtain a flat and even piece of felt, around 5 mm thick.

3. Allow the felt to dry.

4. Trace the cloud motif from page 68 and cut it out, then put the paper pattern on the felt and cut around its outline. This will give you a cloud with rough edges.

5. Use the felting needle to prick around the edges of the cloud and make it smooth (see *Tips & Techniques*, page 6).

CLOUD BROOCH

(continued)

6. Add the decoration to the cloud: take a few small pieces of coloured wool and use your fingers to roll them into little balls (for the red cloud) or oval shapes (for the blue cloud). Arrange them in place and prick with the felting needle to attach them to the cloud. Jab repeatedly on the same spot until they are securely joined to the white cloud.

7. The dangling raindrops are made from small pieces of coloured wool (to make pale blue raindrops, mix blue and white wool together with soap and hot water). Roll each piece into a ball in the palm of your hand and then needle-felt it to form three raindrop shapes, in slightly different sizes.

8. Thread the needle and use tiny stitches to sew the raindrops onto the bottom edge of the cloud, arranging them in a row from smallest to largest.

9. Sew the brooch clip onto the back of the cloud.

SPEECH BUBBLES

Level of difficulty
Easy

Time required
1 hr + drying time

Technique
Modelling clay + transfer

Materials
Air-drying modelling
  clay or cold porcelain
  in white
Sharp knife
Fine sandpaper (P400
  grade)
Pencil
Tracing paper
Ballpoint pen
Fine paintbrush
Black acrylic paint
Matt spray varnish for
  acrylic paint
2 brooch clips, 3 cm long
Two-part epoxy glue

Say what you have to say without opening your mouth!

Instructions

1. Trace the speech bubble motifs from page 68 onto paper and cut them out.

2. Make a ball of modelling clay in the palm of your hand. Flatten it and place the template for one speech bubble on top of it. Use the tip of the knife to cut out the shape of the bubble. Do the same with the second bubble.

3. To make the bubbles flat, moisten the blade of the knife and gently smooth it over the surface of the bubbles several times. Leave the bubbles to dry.

4. Sand the surfaces of the bubbles to obtain a smooth, flat surface.

5. Trace the outlines of the lettering from page 68 in pencil, then fill in the letters, again in pencil, on the reverse side of the tracing paper.

6. Place the tracing paper over the bubble, with the filled-in side facing down, then go over the top side of each letter carefully, this time with the ballpoint pen. The lettering will end up printed on the bubble (see *Tips & Techniques*, page 6).

7. Use the paintbrush to paint over the letters with the black acrylic paint.

8. Spray two coats of varnish on the bubbles.

9. Glue a brooch clip to the back of each bubble.

PENCIL BUTTERFLY

Level of difficulty
Difficult

Time required
1½ hrs

Technique
Woodwork + glue

Materials
4 fluorescent pencils
  (yellow, pink, green
  and orange)
Hacksaw or mini circular
  saw
Contact glue
2 fabric flower stamens
  in black waxed cotton,
  with beaded ends
1 brooch clip, 4 cm long

This brightly coloured butterfly is a real eye-catcher.

Instructions

1. Use the hacksaw or circular saw to cut slices of pencil, each 0.7 cm thick, as follows: 8 yellow pieces; 6 orange pieces; 9 pink pieces; 6 green pieces.

2. Arrange the pencil pieces in the pattern shown in diagrams **Ⓐ** and **Ⓑ** below. Glue the pencil blocks together, one wing at a time. Before gluing the two forewings together, slide the base of the flower stamens between them so that they will be held in place, forming the butterfly's antennae.

3. Glue the hindwings to the forewings, as indicated in diagram **Ⓑ** below.

4. Glue a brooch clip onto the back of the butterfly.

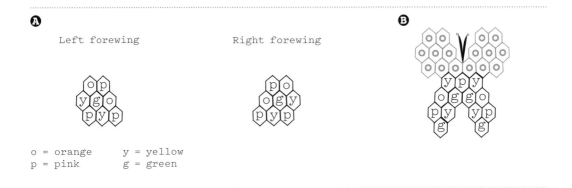

Ⓐ

Left forewing   Right forewing   **Ⓑ**

o = orange   y = yellow
p = pink   g = green

STAR-STUDDED SPIRAL

Level of difficulty
Easy

Time required
1 hr

Technique
Gluing + sewing

Materials
Olive green tissue paper
Gold tissue paper
Turquoise tissue paper
Navy blue tissue paper
Mint green tissue paper
PVA glue
Broad paintbrush
Tulle netting
Scissors
Pencil
Ruler
1 piece of wire, 31 cm
  long
1 piece of black PVC
  craft tubing, 31 cm
  long
1 brooch clip, 2 cm long
Two-part epoxy glue

Choose matching colours for this constellation of stars - or try some bold contrasts instead!

Instructions

1. To prepare the tissue paper, first dilute the PVA glue with water so that it's not too thick. Cut a 7 × 7 cm square from each of the five colours of tissue paper. Brush each square with the glue and stick them all onto the net backing. Leave to dry.

2. Trace the two star motifs from page 69 and cut them out. Draw two large stars on the olive green, mint green and turquoise paper, and two small stars on the gold and navy blue paper. Cut out all ten stars.

3. Take one star of each colour and fold it as shown in diagram **Ⓐ** below. Give the stars shape by pinching the folded edges to create volume.

4. Apply glue to the back of each unfolded star and stick it to the back of the folded star of the same colour.

Ⓐ

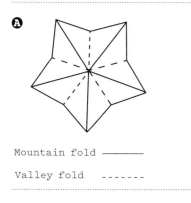

Mountain fold ———

Valley fold - - - - - -

STAR-STUDDED SPIRAL

(continued)

B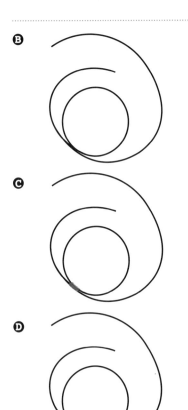

5. Thread the wire inside the plastic tubing to stiffen it. Shape it into a spiral, as shown in diagram **B**.

6. Stitch the overlapping sections of plastic tube together, at the point shown in diagram **C**.

7. Sew the brooch clip onto the underside of the spiral, as shown in diagram **D**.

8. Stick the stars onto the right side of the spiral with epoxy glue, as shown in diagram **E**.

Underside of the spiral

E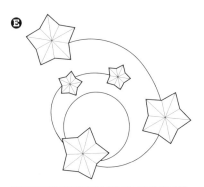

FOX BROOCH

Level of difficulty
Easy

Time required
30 mins

Technique
Origami

Materials
Orange tissue paper
  (or other lightweight
  paper)
Tulle netting
PVA glue
White acrylic paint
Fine paintbrush
Black acrylic paint
1 brooch clip, 4 cm long
Two-part epoxy glue

This distinctive red fox has a very modern look.

Instructions

1. Cut out a 10 × 10 cm square of tissue paper, then use the PVA glue to stick it onto a 10.5 × 10.5 cm square of tulle netting, as shown in diagram **Ⓐ**.

2. Fold the square as indicated in diagram **Ⓑ** below and diagram **Ⓒ** overleaf to make a fox.

3. Paint the fox's muzzle with white acrylic paint, then paint its eyes and nose with black acrylic paint.

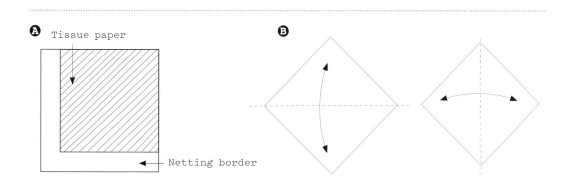

Ⓐ Tissue paper

← Netting border

Ⓑ

FOX BROOCH
(continued)

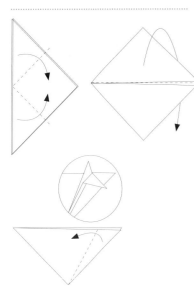

4. Make the fox's tail: trace the template on page 69 and cut it out, then draw and cut out two copies of this shape from the tissue paper and two from the netting. Layer these shapes over each other, alternating paper and netting, then fan them out slightly to add volume to the tail, as shown in diagram **C**. Use the PVA glue to stick these elements together.

5. Stick the tail to the fox's body.

6. Use the epoxy glue to fix the brooch clip to the back of the fox.

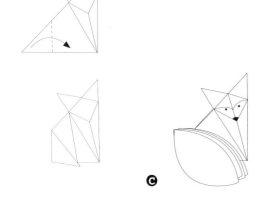

C

PAPER HEART

Level of difficulty
Medium

Time required
1½ hrs

Technique
Paper cutting

Materials
Grey cardboard,
  2 mm thick
Pencil
Ruler
Craft knife
White paper with gold
  polka dots
PVA glue and brush
Heavy black paper
  (at least 250 gsm)
1 brooch clip, 2.5 cm
  long
Two-part epoxy glue

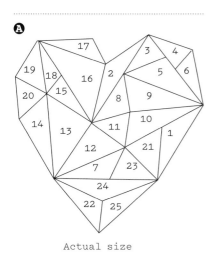

Actual size

**Piece together this paper heart and
wear it close to your own.**

Instructions

1. Trace the heart template from
page 69, including the lines inside
it. Cut out the heart, draw around it
on the grey cardboard. Cut out the
cardboard heart and trace the inner
lines onto it.

2. Use the craft knife to score
along the lines inside the heart, as
indicated in diagram **A**, so that you
can fold the card without breaking it.

3. Transfer all the triangles on
the template onto another piece of
cardboard and cut them all out. Number
each triangle on the reverse, so that
you will know where they go when you
stick them together.

4. Cover all the cardboard triangles
with dotted paper, sticking it down
with PVA glue. Make sure you cover
the edges.

5. Stick each triangle in position on
the cardboard heart. Once they are all
pasted in place, gently shape the base
to highlight the cracks between the
triangles.

6. Place the heart on the thick black
paper and draw around it. Cut out the
shape, then paste it on the back of
the heart.

7. When everything is dry, use the
epoxy glue to stick the brooch clip
onto the back of the heart.

31

ORIGAMI BROOCH

Level of difficulty
Difficult

Time required
1 hr

Technique
Embossed aluminium

Materials
Grey cardboard,
  2 mm thick
Pencil
Ruler
Scissors
3 sheets of aluminium
  embossing foil
  (220 × 163 mm)
Two-part epoxy glue
Bone folder
Embossing tool with
  a small ball end
Black paper (at least
  110 gsm)
1 brooch clip, 3.5 cm long

These simple origami shapes are easy to make from paper, but this embossed metal version will brighten up any outfit.

Instructions

1. Trace the three shapes on page 69 onto paper and cut them out. Draw around them on the grey cardboard and then cut out the shapes.

2. Glue the cardboard pieces onto the embossing foil, leaving a border of 1.5 cm around each one. Cut out the pieces, including the border.

3. Apply glue along the edges of the cardboard and use the bone folder to fold over the aluminium borders. On piece C, you should only fold two sides over, as shown in diagram **Ⓐ**.

Ⓐ

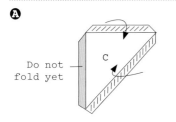

Do not fold yet — C

ORIGAMI BROOCH

(continued)

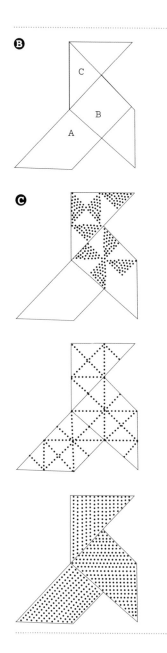

4. Using the epoxy glue, stick piece B over piece A, then piece C over piece B, as shown in diagram **B**. Then fold down the final flap of piece C, joining C and B together.

5. Now that all three pieces are joined together, use the embossing tool to decorate the brooch, drawing inspiration from the ideas shown in diagram **C**. Work carefully, so that you emboss the metal without making holes in it.

6. Place the brooch on the black paper, draw around it and cut it out. Carefully stick the paper shape onto the back of the brooch.

7. Glue the clip onto the back of the brooch.

VINTAGE-STYLE BADGES

Level of difficulty
Easy

Time required
2 hrs + drying time

Technique
Transfer printing

Materials
Image transfer medium,
   such as Transcryl®
   (see page 7)
Flat paintbrush
3 white board-game
   counters, 3.5 cm in
   diameter
Matt varnish spray
Craft drill with a very
   fine bit
Tracing paper
Fine paintbrush
Black acrylic paint
3 brooch clips, 2 cm long
Two-part epoxy glue

Make your own badges by transfer-printing these delicate rustic motifs.

Instructions for the Tree and Penny Farthing badges

1. Photocopy designs 1 and 2 from page 69.

2. Use the flat paintbrush to apply several coats of the image transfer medium onto the back of the photocopied designs. Wait for 15 to 20 mins between each layer so that it can dry. Switch the direction of your brushstrokes each time: apply a coat horizontally, leave to dry, apply another coat vertically, leave to dry, etc. Repeat this process at least five times.

3. After leaving to dry for 24 hours, cut round the design, allowing a border of 0.3 cm, then plunge it into warm water so that it peels away easily.

4. Peel the paper off the back of the print by rubbing it gently and separating it from the plastic film. Leave to dry.

5. Stick the film onto the centre of one of the counters by applying a layer of transfer medium to the back of the transfer and pasting it down while wet, making sure you press out any air bubbles carefully. Leave to dry.

6. Spray on several thin layers of matt varnish.

7. Use the epoxy glue to stick a brooch clip to the back of each badge.

VINTAGE-STYLE BADGES

(continued)

Instructions for the Leaf badge

1. Trace design 3 from page 69, then go over the back of the drawing with the pencil. Position the motif pencilled side downwards in the centre of a games counter. Go over the drawing with a ballpoint pen to print the drawing onto the counter.

2. Use the craft drill to make holes along all the lines of the drawing, creating shallow grooves that do not perforate the counter completely.

3. Use the fine paintbrush to go over all the pencil lines with black acrylic paint.

4. Spray on several thin layers of matt varnish.

5. Use the epoxy glue to stick a brooch clip to the back of the badge.

AMPERSAND BROOCH

Level of difficulty
Medium

Time required
1 hr

Technique
Glue + cutting

Materials
Grey cardboard,
  2 mm thick
Pencil
Scissors
Green velvet
Contact glue
Green metal zip,
  20 cm long
Black felt
Black cotton or
  polyester thread
Needle
1 brooch clip, 4 cm long

An ampersand jumps off the page and onto your lapel.

Instructions

1. Trace the ampersand motif from page 70 and transfer it onto the cardboard. Carefully cut around its outline and the inner spaces.

2. Use the contact glue to stick the cardboard shape on the back of the velvet, right side down. Cut out the velvet, leaving a border of 1 cm around the outer edge of the cardboard shape.

3. Use the scissors to make notches in the fabric border, 1 cm apart, as shown in diagram **Ⓐ**.

4. Apply glue to the edges of the cardboard ampersand and fold over the edges of the velvet to stick them down.

5. Open the zip, then cut it into two lengthwise and remove the ends.

6. Apply glue to the outer edges of the ampersand and position the zip around the edge, with the metal teeth pointing downwards. Stick it down carefully, holding the zip in place with your fingers as you do so. Do the same for the holes in the middle.

7. Use the scissors to make notches in the fabric section of the zip, then apply glue and stick it to the back.

8. Cut an ampersand out of the felt and stick it on the back of the velvet ampersand.

9. Sew the clip onto the back of the brooch.

Ⓐ

SQUIRREL BROOCH

Level of difficulty
Medium

Time required
1½ hrs

Technique
Paper + glue

Materials
Tracing paper
Pencil
Ballpoint pen
Grey cardboard,
  2 mm thick
Craft knife
Lightweight red paper
  (80 gsm)
PVA glue
Fine paintbrush
Scraps of paper, in
  various colours
1 black seed bead
Two-part epoxy glue
Heavy black paper
  (300 gsm)
1 brooch clip, 4 cm long

This brooch is not particularly difficult to make, but the cutting and gluing take time. Experiment with different coloured papers to add sparkle to the squirrel's tail.

Instructions

1. Trace the squirrel motif from page 70 and then go over it in pencil on the reverse side. Place this side of the tracing paper on the grey cardboard, then go over the drawing with the ballpoint pen to transfer it onto the grey cardboard.

2. Cut out the shape carefully with the craft knife.

3. Apply PVA glue to the cardboard shape and place it on top of the red paper. Draw around the squirrel shape, leaving a 0.5 cm border. Apply glue to the edges of the cardboard and the red paper border, then fold the border over and stick it down.

4. Cut the coloured paper scraps into strips 0.3 cm and 0.5 cm wide. Cut these strips into pieces 1.5 cm long.

5. Put a little dot of glue on the end of each piece of paper and begin to stick them down, layering them as indicated in diagram **Ⓐ**. Start at the top of the tail, then cover the back leg before moving up the body. Finish with the head. Each new piece of paper should partially overlap the previous one. Try to create an interesting interplay of colours as you work.

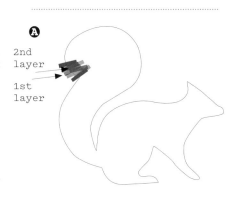

Ⓐ

2nd
layer

1st
layer

SQUIRREL BROOCH

(continued)

6. Stick a black seed bead onto the head to form the squirrel's eye.

7. Use the tracing paper to copy the outline of the squirrel onto the black paper, then cut it out and stick it onto the back of the cardboard squirrel with PVA glue.

8. Use the epoxy glue to stick the brooch clip to the back of the brooch.

ABSTRACT GARDEN

Level of difficulty
Medium

Time required
2½ hrs

Technique
Woodwork, metalwork +
  cold porcelain

Materials
1 piece of dark wood
  (e.g. ebony), 10 × 3 cm
Mini circular saw or
  small craft saw
Fine bradawl
15 g of cold porcelain
Craft knife
2 bright green
  paper clips
Cutting pliers
Needle
1 brooch clip, 4 cm long
Two-part epoxy glue
Sandpaper (grades P400
  and P150)
Contact glue

A delicate, poetic brooch.

Instructions

1. First make the black base. Transfer the template on page 70 onto the wood and cut out the rectangle with the saw. Sand down the edges to obtain a long, smooth oval, as shown in diagram **Ⓐ**.

2. Use the bradawl to make five holes in the upper edge of the wooden base, using diagram **Ⓑ** overleaf as a guide.

3. Use your fingers to mould three little balls with the cold porcelain. Leave them to dry. Make three more shapes the size of coffee beans. Squash them between your fingers to form an oval. Make an indent in the centre of each one with the craft knife, as shown in diagram **Ⓒ** overleaf, then leave them to dry.

4. Use the pliers to cut the paper clips, paying attention to their curves. Use diagram **Ⓓ** overleaf as a guide.

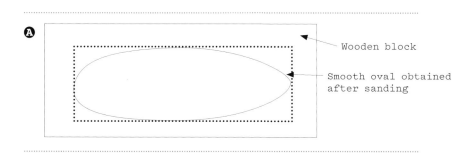

Ⓐ

Wooden block

Smooth oval obtained
after sanding

ABSTRACT GARDEN

(continued)

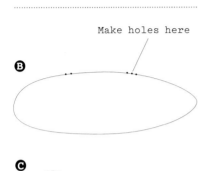

Make holes here

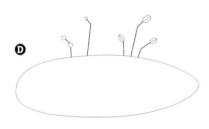

5. Use the needle to gently pierce the cold porcelain balls. Then put a drop of contact glue into each hole and thread each ball onto a paper-clip stem, as shown in diagram **D**. Repeat this process for the rest of the flowers.

6. Use the epoxy glue to stick the clip to the back of the brooch.

OAK LEAF BROOCH

Level of difficulty
Medium

Time required
2 hrs

Technique
Embossing

Materials
Tracing paper
1 sheet of aluminium
    embossing foil
Pencil
Scissors
Embossing tool with
    a ball end
Embossing tool with
    a pointed end
Surgical spirit
Two-part epoxy glue
6 cm of wire, 1 mm in
    diameter
Orange or yellow glass
    paint
Fine paintbrush
1 brooch clip, 4 cm long

Colourful autumn leaves are always enchanting.

Instructions

1. Trace the leaf motif from page 70. Transfer two copies of its outline onto the embossing foil and cut them out with the scissors.

2. Copy the dot and line motifs shown on the template onto the back of one of the leaves. Use the pointed embossing tool to score along the veins, pressing on the leaf to emboss the metal. Work slowly, to avoid deviating from the line. Then use the ball-ended tool to firmly press all the dots, without perforating the foil but hard enough to leave a mark.

3. To join the two leaves together, first clean the two inner surfaces with surgical spirit, making sure to remove any grease. Then apply epoxy glue to the back of one of the leaves. Before gluing it to the other leaf, slide the wire stem between the leaves, then leave to dry.

4. Apply two coats of glass paint to both sides of the leaf with the fine paintbrush, along with the stem. Allow the first coat to dry before applying the second.

5. Clean the brooch clip with the surgical spirit, then glue it to the back of the leaf with the epoxy glue.

BOW TIE BROOCH

Level of difficulty
Easy

Time required
30 mins

Technique
Leather work

Materials
Lightweight green or
  white leather
Pencil
Scissors
Pinking shears
Hole punch, 0.5 cm in
  diameter
Contact glue for fabric
  and leather
Two-part epoxy glue
1 brooch clip, 3 cm long

This miniature bow tie is both elegant and whimsical. It works well in any colour and for any occasion.

Instructions

1. Copy the bow tie and ribbon templates from page 71 and transfer them onto the leather of your choice. Cut out the shapes with the scissors (if you want to make the version with zigzag edging, use pinking shears).

2. To make the polka-dot variation, position the hole punch over the wings of the bow tie and press firmly all over the leather to dot it with circles, making sure that you do not cut all the way through.

3. For all of the designs, pinch the leather ends inwards and fix them with contact glue, as shown in diagram **A**.

4. Turn the bow tie over and fold each wing into the centre, as shown in diagram **B**. Use the contact glue to stick the two folded ends in place, one alongside the other.

5. Wrap the leather ribbon around the middle of the bow tie and glue it in place. Try using a different shade of leather for the ribbon, or even a different material.

6. Use the epoxy glue to stick a clip to the back of the brooch.

Ⓐ

Right side of
the leather

Pinch the leather inwards
at both ends and glue.

Ⓑ

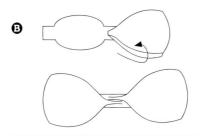

PEBBLE HEART

Level of difficulty
Easy

Time required
30 mins

Technique
Painting + gluing

Materials
Small, flat pebbles
White acrylic paint
Fine paintbrush
Two-part epoxy glue
Brooch clips (in a size
that matches the
pebbles)

A few pebbles from a beach can easily become a striking holiday souvenir.

Instructions

Design 1

1. Stick two flat pebbles together to form a heart shape.

2. Using a fine brush, paint two oval shapes with diluted white acrylic paint, as shown in diagram **Ⓐ**.

3. Paint a dotted line around the oval shapes with undiluted white paint.

Design 2

1. Stick two flat pebbles together to form a heart shape.

2. Paint a dotted line with white acrylic paint to form a heart that spreads across both pebbles.

Whichever design you choose, use the epoxy glue to stick on a brooch clip.

Designs

Ⓐ

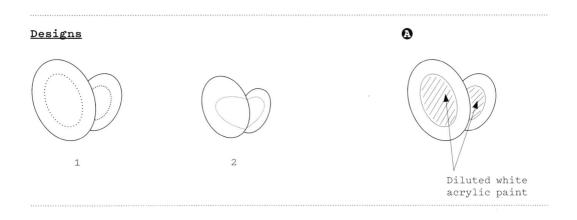

1

2

Diluted white
acrylic paint

PATTERNED PEBBLES

Level of difficulty
Easy

Time required
30 mins

Technique
Embossing + gluing

Materials
Small, flat pebbles
Hole puncher, 0.5 cm
    in diameter
1 sheet of aluminium
    embossing foil
Embossing tool with a
    pointed end
Two-part epoxy glue
Scissors
Brooch clips (in a size
    that matches the
    pebbles)

Designs

Polka dots   Stars

Polka-dot design

1. Use the hole puncher to make small round pieces of the embossing foil.

2. Use the epoxy glue to paste them onto a pebble. Shape the aluminium pieces before gluing them down: aluminium is flexible, so you can press it firmly to fit the contours of the pebble.

Star design

1. Trace the star motif from page 71 and transfer it onto embossing foil. Repeat this process four more times and cut out all five stars with the scissors.

2. Use the pointed embossing tool to press little dots into one side of the star. Stick the stars on the pebble as shown in the diagram below. As with the polka dots above, shape the stars to fit the pebble's surface before sticking them down.

Whichever design you choose, use the epoxy glue to stick on a brooch clip matching the size of the pebble.

MEDAL BROOCH

Level of difficulty
Medium

Time required
1½ hrs + drying time

Technique
Crochet + modelling clay

Materials
Air-drying modelling
  clay in white
Tulle netting
Large snap fastener
Embossing tool with a
  pointed end
Pink polyester thread
Silver polyester thread
Needle
Small metal crochet hook
1 brooch clip, 4 cm long

This pretty brooch requires some basic crochet skills.

Instructions

1. Make a small ball of modelling clay, then squash it until you end up with a fairly regular disc 0.3 cm thick and about 2.5 cm in diameter.

2. Reproduce the texture of the netting by placing it on top of the modelling clay and pressing gently. Remove the netting. Reproduce the shape of the snap fastener by pressing it into the centre of the disc. Remove the fastener, then leave the disc to dry.

3. Use the embossing tool to make an even row of small holes around the edge of the disc.

4. Crochet with the pink and silver threads, as shown in diagram **Ⓐ**.

Pass one pink and one silver thread through the first hole, make a loop with them and crochet three chain stitches. Then pass the two threads through the next hole and crochet another three chain stitches; continue until you have worked all the way around the disc. On the second round, crochet five times into the gap left by the three chain stitches of the first round. On the third round, crochet eight chain stitches between each pair of holes. When the third round is complete, pass the thread through the final loop and tie it off in a knot.

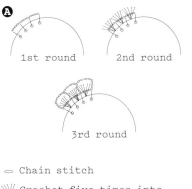

Ⓐ

1st round   2nd round

3rd round

◯ Chain stitch

⋁ Crochet five times into
  the same stitch

MEDAL BROOCH

(continued)

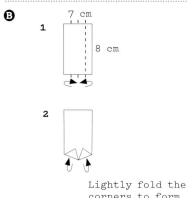

1

7 cm

8 cm

2

Lightly fold the
corners to form
a point

Fold the upper edge downwards

3

C

5. Cut out a piece of tulle netting measuring 7 × 8 cm. Fold in each side to meet the centre line, as shown in diagram **B**. Fold in the bottom corners to make a shallow point, then fold the top edge downwards.

6. Thread a needle with silver thread and stitch little dots at regular intervals all over the tulle, as shown in diagram **C**.

7. Sew the medal onto the bottom point of the tulle ribbon with a few stitches in silver thread.

8. Sew the clip on the back of the brooch, at the top of the tulle ribbon.

FOUR-LEAF CLOVER

Level of difficulty
Easy

Time required
1 hr

Technique
Embossed paper +
  metalwork

Materials
Heavy black paper
  (300 gsm)
Pencil
Embossing tool with
  a small ball end
Ruler
1 sheet of aluminium
  embossing foil
Scissors
Two-part epoxy glue
Gilded copper wire,
  0.4 mm in diameter
Gilded copper wire,
  1 mm in diameter
Cutting pliers
1 gold kilt pin, 5 cm
  long

Ⓐ

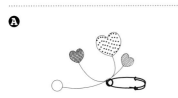

**A lucky charm that can be worn all
year round!**

Instructions

1. Trace the three heart motifs from
page 71 and transfer two copies of
each onto the black paper. Cut them
out. Mark the lines and dots on all six
sides of the hearts with the embossing
tool - don't press too hard, but use
enough pressure to emboss the paper.
Use the ruler as a guide when drawing
the lines, and make sure that the dots
are spaced regularly.

2. Cut out two circles, 1.5 cm in
diameter, from the embossing foil.

3. Take the 1-mm copper wire and cut
two stems, each 7 cm long.

4. Glue two matching hearts to each end
of the first stem. Glue two matching
hearts to one end of the second stem
and the two aluminium circles to the
other end.

5. Bend the first stem in half, folding
it around the second stem. Use the
0.4-mm copper wire to bind the two
stems to each other and to the end of
the kilt pin, as shown in diagram **Ⓐ**.

JELLYFISH BROOCH

Level of difficulty
Difficult

Time required
2 hrs

Technique
Embossing

Materials
Heavy black paper
  (300 gsm)
Grey cardboard,
  2 mm thick
1 sheet of aluminium
  embossing foil
Pair of compasses
Scissors
Embossing tool with
  a small ball end
Ruler
Two-part epoxy glue
Gilded copper wire,
  0.4 mm in diameter
Gilded copper wire,
  1 mm in diameter
Silver crimp beads
Thin, pointed pliers
1 brooch clip, 4 cm long
Contact glue

This half-moon brooch is reminiscent of a jellyfish with beaded tentacles.

Instructions

1. Using the compasses, draw a semi-circle, 6 cm in diameter, on the black paper and cut it out with the scissors. Draw a semi-circle 5.5 cm in diameter on the grey cardboard and cut it out too.

2. Use the embossing tool to make rows of dots on the thick black paper as shown in diagram **Ⓐ**, using the ruler as a guide.

3. Use contact glue to stick the indented side of the black semi-circle to the grey cardboard, leaving a 0.5-cm border of black paper. Cut tabs in the black paper as shown in diagram **Ⓑ**, then fold down the tabs and glue them to the cardboard.

4. Cut six pieces of 0.4-mm copper wire: one 3 cm long; two 5 cm long; two 6 cm long; and one 7 cm long. Use the pliers to fix a few silver crimp beads onto each piece of wire, roughly 1 cm apart.

5. Stick the copper wires to the back of the black semi-circle with sticky tape, as shown in diagram **Ⓒ** on page 67.

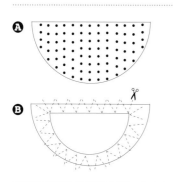

JELLYFISH BROOCH

(continued)

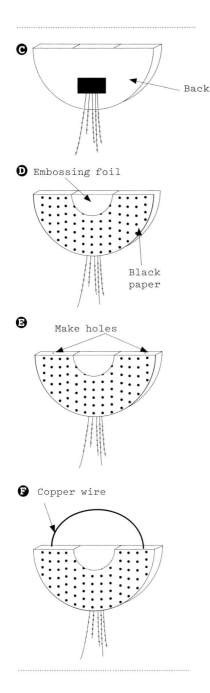

C

Back

D Embossing foil

Black paper

E Make holes

F Copper wire

6. Draw and cut out a semi-circle of black paper, 5.5 cm in diameter, and stick it on the back of the brooch with contact glue.

7. Draw and cut out a semi-circle of embossing foil, 2.5 cm in diameter. Fold it over the upper edge of the black brooch, centring it as shown in diagram **D**, and stick it in position with epoxy glue.

8. Use a needle to make two holes on the top edge of the brooch, each 1.5 cm from the end, as indicated in diagram **E**.

9. Take the 1-mm copper wire and cut a piece 8.5 cm long. Put epoxy glue on the ends and stick them into the holes you have just made, as shown in diagram **F**. Hold the curved wire in place until the glue hardens.

10. Stick the clip to the back of the brooch with epoxy glue.

TEMPLATES & MOTIFS

Moustache brooch
(page 12)

Right
side

5 mm clear border
around the edge

Actual size

Cloud brooch
(page 15)

Actual size

Speech
bubbles
(page 19)

Keep
calm!

and
smile :)

Actual size

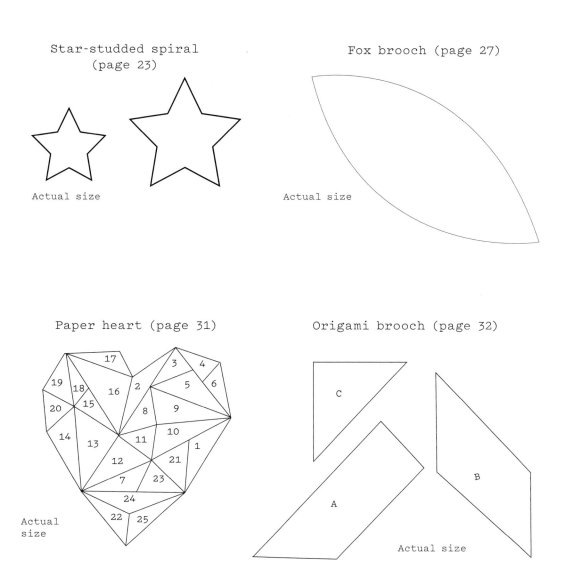

Star-studded spiral
(page 23)

Actual size

Fox brooch (page 27)

Actual size

Paper heart (page 31)

17
19
18   16   2
20   15   5   6
14   8   9
13   11   10
12   1
7   23   21
24
22   25

Actual
size

Origami brooch (page 32)

C

A   B

Actual size

Vintage-style badges (page 36)

1) Tree   2) Penny farthing   3) Leaf

Ampersand brooch (page 40)

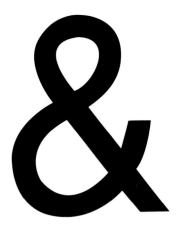

Actual size

Squirrel brooch (page 43)

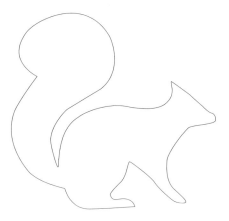

Actual size

Abstract garden (page 47)

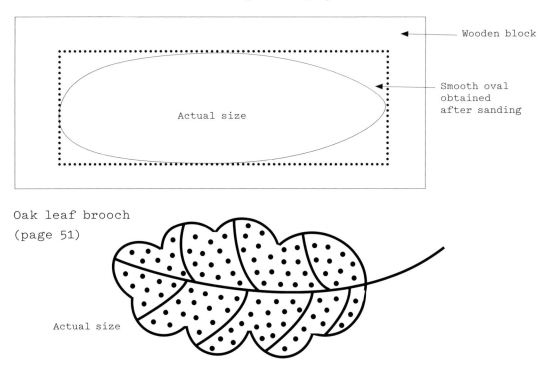

Wooden block

Smooth oval obtained after sanding

Actual size

Oak leaf brooch (page 51)

Actual size

Bow tie brooch (page 52)

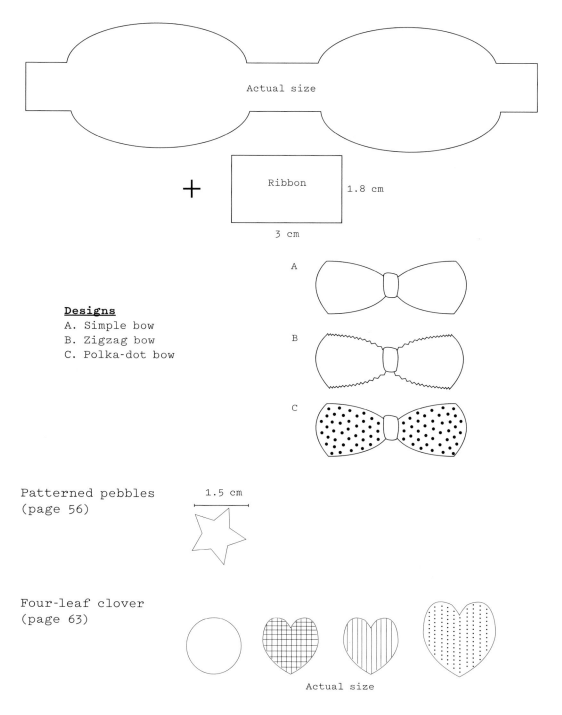

Actual size

Ribbon

1.8 cm

3 cm

+

A

Designs
A. Simple bow
B. Zigzag bow
C. Polka-dot bow

B

C

Patterned pebbles
(page 56)

1.5 cm

Four-leaf clover
(page 63)

Actual size

USEFUL ADDRESSES

Craft Cellar
www.craftcellar.co.uk
For modelling clays, embossing foils and more

London Graphic Centre
www.londongraphics.co.uk

Minerva Crafts
www.minervacrafts.com
An extensive range of fabrics and sewing equipment

Shepherds of London
www.bookbinding.co.uk
A good source for decorative paper and art supplies

World of Wool
www.worldofwool.co.uk
For wool, ready-made felt and felting supplies

Translated from the French *Les petits ateliers Hachette: Broches*
by Matthew Clarke

First published in the United Kingdom in 2016 by
Thames & Hudson Ltd, 181A High Holborn, London WC1V 7QX

Original edition © 2015 Hachette Livre (Hachette Pratique), Paris
This edition © 2016 Thames & Hudson Ltd, London

British Library Cataloguing-in-Publication Data
A catalogue record for this book is available from the British Library

ISBN 978-0-500-51844-1

Printed in Spain

To find out about all our publications, please visit **www.thamesandhudson.com**.
There you can subscribe to our e-newsletter, browse or download our current catalogue,
and buy any titles that are in print.